...ished
...ands,
...ravel.

...our
...rets
...orld,
...n of
...nce and a passion for travel.

**Rely on Thomas Cook as your
travelling companion on your next trip
and benefit from our unique heritage.**

Thomas Cook **pocket** guides

SHEFFIELD

Written by Robert Savage

Published by Thomas Cook Publishing
A division of Thomas Cook Tour Operations Limited
Company registration no. 3772199 England
The Thomas Cook Business Park, Unit 9, Coningsby Road,
Peterborough PE3 8SB, United Kingdom
Email: books@thomascook.com, Tel: +44 (0) 1733 416477
www.thomascookpublishing.com

Produced by Cambridge Publishing Management Limited
Burr Elm Court, Main Street, Caldecote CB23 7NU
www.cambridgepm.co.uk

ISBN: 978-1-84848-470-2

This first edition © 2011 Thomas Cook Publishing
Text © Thomas Cook Publishing
Cartography supplied by Redmoor Design, Tavistock, Devon
Map data © OpenStreetMap contributors CC-BY-SA, www.openstreetmap.org,
www.creativecommons.org
Transport map © Stagecoach Supertram Ltd

Series Editor: Karen Beaulah
Production/DTP: Steven Collins

Printed and bound in Spain by GraphyCems

Cover photography © Thomas Cook Publishing

CONTENTS

SYMBOLS KEY

The following symbols are used throughout this book:

ⓐ address ❶ telephone ⓦ website address ⓔ email
🕒 opening times Ⓝ public transport connections ❶ important

The following symbols are used on the maps:

🄸 information office		■ point of interest	
✈ airport		○ city	
➕ hospital		○ large town	
🄲 police station		○ village or small town	
🚌 bus station		═ motorway	
🚆 railway station		─ main road	
🅣 tram		─ minor road	
✝ cathedral		─ railway	

❶ numbers denote featured cafés, restaurants & venues

PRICE CATEGORIES

The ratings below indicate average price rates for a double
room per night, including breakfast:
£ up to £49 ££ £50–99 £££ over £100
The typical cost for a three-course meal without drinks
is as follows:
£ up to £20 ££ £20–30 £££ over £30

▶ *Millennium Square fountains and the Winter Garden*

 INTRODUCING
Sheffield

Introduction

Sheffield might be known to many for its industrial past and Dennis Taylor's spectacles, but there's much more to this city than steel and snooker players. The city takes its name from the River Sheaf and the Anglo-Saxon name for a treeless area surrounded by woods (*feld*), and was founded more than 1,000 years ago.

It's not a city that you can compare with the likes of Paris, Rome or Madrid because it's an entirely different kind of animal, but it is a great British city with a lot to offer to anyone who decides to visit. When you arrive in Sheffield, expect a warm welcome, people who make eye contact and smile, a sense of pride in the clean and regularly swept city streets, and of course a healthy dose of Yorkshire wit.

The city has come a long way in the last 20 years and a great deal of it has been redeveloped beyond recognition. However, around every corner you will see a vestige of Sheffield's rich and diverse heritage.

Whether it's the scars left over from the World War II bombs that damaged the City Hall during the Sheffield Blitz or the bronze statue of Vulcan, the Roman god of fire and furnaces, on top of the Town Hall representing Sheffield's steel industry, there's an interesting tale behind everything in the city.

Add to this two world-class universities, a reputation for medical excellence at the teaching hospital, a burgeoning boutique shopping strip, internationally acclaimed sporting events, art galleries galore and a theatre scene that boasts the best productions from London's West End, and you have an idea of what to expect when you arrive in Sheffield.

There's much more here than what many saw portrayed in the film *The Full Monty*, and the people of the city are understandably very proud of their particular patch of South Yorkshire. When you get to know the city for what it is today and for its role in the history of the UK, you'll understand why.

▲ *The water cascade and steel sculpture, Sheaf Square*

When to go

From the famous World Snooker Championship to the relatively new Sheffield Adventure Film Festival, you're guaranteed to find something to entertain you whenever you're in the city. The autumn and winter weather is comparable to that of Manchester – making an umbrella an essential companion – but in the summer the hillside location works to the city's advantage, with comfortable temperatures long after the sun sets.

ANNUAL EVENTS

Major sporting and cultural events take place in Sheffield throughout the year. The **Aviva World Trials** and the **UK Indoor Championships** are some of the biggest events in the UK Athletics diary. They're both held at the English Institute of Sport over a weekend in February. The **Sheffield Adventure Film Festival** is held at the Showroom Cinema. Affectionately known as **ShAFF**, this annual event plays out over a weekend in early March.

The **World Snooker Championship** is undoubtedly the best-known event on the Sheffield calendar. It traditionally runs during the second half of April and into May, at the Crucible. The **FINA Diving World Series** also comes to town in April. This takes place at the Ponds Forge International Sports Centre and, compared to the snooker, it's a good deal easier to get tickets.

The **May Day** celebrations are a big deal in Sheffield, and include everything from morris dancers in the city centre to charity treks into the Peak District. The **Sheffield Half Marathon** and the **Great Fun Race** are also permanent fixtures in late April and early May.

The open-air concerts at the **Don Valley Stadium** are the stuff of legend and when Tina Turner played here in the late 1990s, the hits belted out could be heard reverberating off the sides of the Don Valley, some 20 miles away. Today the stages here and at the neighbouring **Sheffield Arena** still attract all the big names on the music, comedy, ice-skating and dance circuits – especially during the summer months.

In the winter months, the international markets descend on the **Barker's Pool** area, with stalls selling the finest food and colourful decorations, and music from some cracking Christmas choirs. The seasonal pantomime at the **Lyceum Theatre** is also a big draw along with the festive ice-skating rink at the **Sheffield Botanical Gardens**.

⏶ *Ponds Forge is built to world and Olympic standards*

History

Just over 1,000 years ago, a small hamlet called Escafeld was established by the river Sheaf. It soon began to prosper and the Castle Market was established, drawing traders to the area. By the 14th century, the natural resources in the surrounding valleys were being used to forge a name in the steel trade. The extensive woodland provided charcoal needed for smelting, the hills were mined for their thick veins of iron ore, local gritstone was quarried for grinding, and the rivers Don, Porter and Sheaf were harnessed to turn the water wheels.

The steel industry really took off when Benjamin Huntsman invented the Crucible steel process in the 18th century; before this, however, Sheffield was known internationally for an entirely different reason. In 1570, Mary, Queen of Scots was imprisoned in Sheffield Castle under the charge of the sixth Earl of Shrewsbury – George Talbot – and his wife Elizabeth, better known as Bess of Hardwick. The castle was destroyed in 1648 at the end of the civil war but its notoriety survived.

As the steel industry grew, so did the population, and in 1843 Sheffield became a borough. By 1888, the number of people living in the area had reached 300,000, making Sheffield a county borough. It became a city in 1893.

Sheffield would later play a crucial role in World War II when the steel industry was called upon to manufacture essential war supplies. The city, however, paid a high price and became the target of many bombing raids. At the end of 1940, in what became known as the Sheffield Blitz, hundreds of lives were lost and scores of buildings were destroyed.

As a result of the extensive war damage many new roads and houses were built and, in the late 50s, a smokeless zone scheme was introduced. This, coupled with the rapid decline of Sheffield's industries in the 1980s, meant that the city became a much cleaner place.

The legacy of the industrial decimation, however, took a lot longer to remedy, but by 1990 the city was getting back on track with the World Student Games, the Meadowhall Shopping Centre and a thriving arts scene all playing an important part in its revival.

◆ *Kelham Island Museum tells Sheffield's industrial story*

Culture

To the world at large, Sheffield's most famous cultural exports include the Arctic Monkeys, The Human League and *The Full Monty*, but beyond this the city is home to a wealth of artistic talent, galleries, museums, theatres, sports facilities and green spaces.

The sense of pride attached to the city's industrial past does of course play a part in how the culture of Sheffield is reflected in its museums. The **Kelham Island Museum** is a prime example of this – showcasing the way in which Sheffield steel changed the face of the city.

Sheffield's diverse arts scene includes everything from the L S Lowry exhibitions at the **Graves Gallery** to the contemporary steel spoon sculptures at the **Millennium Gallery**. Between the **Crucible**, the **Studio** and the **Lyceum**, theatrical offerings include the best local talent, touring shows and opera.

Musically speaking, the city's stages attract the best international acts. As for the local sports culture, Sheffield is home to two major football teams as well as the **Sheffield Steelers** ice hockey team and basketball champions the **Sheffield Tigers**.

The green spaces in the city are also a crucial component in Sheffield's cultural make-up and even when it's too wet to enjoy the great outdoors, visitors can still enjoy the sheltered and welcoming **Winter Garden**.

◗ *Sheffield Cathedral and its Supertram stop*

 # MAKING THE MOST OF
Sheffield

Shopping

Unlike many other cities where shopping centres open on the outskirts and the traditional high street falls into disrepair, thriving Sheffield has benefitted from the best of both worlds.

WHERE TO SHOP

Shopaholics from across Yorkshire are drawn to Sheffield by the efficient infrastructure built around the Meadowhall Shopping Centre and this in turn feeds the city centre, three miles away, via a tram link. It's feasible for shoppers to reach Meadowhall by car, bus or train, make the most of more than 270 indoor shops, hop on a Supertram and be among the shops of the city centre 20 minutes later.

In Sheffield city centre, the department stores and big names cluster around Fargate, a pedestrianised area at the heart of the city, where you can also find the Orchard Square Shopping Centre, a courtyard containing a good selection of shopping opportunities.

A short walk away from the centre are the student shops and boutique vendors of West Street and Division Street, and slighter further afield, Ecclesall Road offers punters a similar mix.

Between the out of town shopping centre and the inner city streets, shoppers are spoilt for choice. But if by any chance you don't happen to find what you're looking for, there's also the outdoor Meadowhall Retail Park close to the Shopping Centre in the Attercliffe area.

MARKETS

Sheffield is also known for the travelling farmers' markets, continental markets and craft markets that set up shop in the Barker's Pool area. There's also a more permanent produce market in Sheffield, close to the canal in the north of the city. Known as the Castle Market, vendors have been selling their wares on this particular spot for nearly 800 years. However, after a multi-million pound redevelopment, the market is to be moved to a brand new home on The Moor, to the south of the city centre.

▲ *Fargate*

Eating & drinking

Sheffield is a veritable hot pot of everything culinary. From some of the best restaurants in Yorkshire to the homely family-run cafés that wouldn't look out of place in *Last of the Summer Wine*, you won't fail to find something to tease your taste buds in this city.

As you'd expect in any city centre, the big-name chain restaurants take precedence, but there's also a generous

● *Relax with a coffee at 22A Norfolk Row*

spattering of unique eateries, serving up local dishes and fusion food – all with a tasty Yorkshire twist!

If you really want to throw yourself into all things local then keep an eye out for the cafés and coffee shops serving up bread-and-butter pudding and Yorkshire curd tarts. A Yorkshire curd tart is just like any other curd tart, but what makes this treat particularly special is the mixture of spices – particularly allspice and nutmeg – added to the filling.

DINING HABITS

In Sheffield your evening meal is called 'tea' – not to be confused with the drink or the dessert course of scones, jam and clotted cream often enjoyed in the afternoon with a cup of tea. Tea is usually served from 18.00 onwards; after 21.00 you might find that the menu selections are a little bit more limited as the restaurant kitchens begin to wind down.

WHERE TO GO

For a quick snack you'll find a good selection of sandwich shops and cafés dotted along **Fargate**'s pedestrianised arteries. **Norfolk Row** and **Tudor Square** are your best bets in this respect.

For something a little more substantial, there is a good selection of restaurants in **Leopold Square**, the open area around the **Peace Gardens** and the stretch of **Division Street** just up from the City Hall.

The **Ecclesall Road** area also offers a good selection of eateries in addition to a number of gastro-pubs, student-chic cafés and fine dining restaurants.

Entertainment

Just like everything else in the city, the entertainment on offer in Sheffield has changed dramatically – as you would expect after two decades of dedicated investment and regeneration. From travelling Ferris wheels stopping off in the city centre to craft fairs in the grand surroundings of the **Millennium Gallery**, Sheffield has a great deal going on.

Whether you have fun for all the family on the agenda or plan to go clubbing into the early hours of the morning, you can rely on Sheffield.

If you fancy a hands-on itinerary and a day of exercise for your mind, the **Magna Science Adventure Centre** is a good bet and one of the few places in the country where you can drive a JCB digger and blow up a rock face – just for fun.

If it's a cultural visit of theatre, museum exhibits and glorious green spaces that you seek, then the offerings around the city, particularly those around Tudor Square, will serve you well.

Musically speaking, the **City Hall** has a good weekly line up. Beyond the bands it's also popular because of **The Last Laugh Comedy Club**, and the classical musicians who belt out Bach in the perfect acoustics of this 2,000-seater auditorium.

Sheffield is also known for its inner city gigs and the eclectic mix of acts playing at the **O₂ Academy**, **The Boardwalk** and the smaller venues dotted along West Street.

If clubbing is your cup of tea then **The Leadmill** and **The Corporation** are the big names in the city; and as for bars, the favourite spots in the centre can found on Division Street and West Street.

The amount of entertainment on offer in the city might appear to be overwhelming, especially when you factor in much more of the same along Ecclesall Road, but it is all worth exploring and you can narrow it down by stopping off at the City Library to pick up a bagful of free event listings and leaflets.

🔺 *Touring shows from London's West End often play at the Lyceum*

Sport & relaxation

CLIMBING

It might not seem like an obvious activity for a city of industry but factor in the many cliff faces and rocky outcrops in the nearby Peak District, and you'll understand why this is such a popular pursuit. The Edge Climbing Centre is a short distance south of the city centre and is the perfect place for experts, and those yet to dip their fingers in the chalk dust. ⓐ John Street ⓣ 0114 275 8899 ⓦ www.sheffieldclimbing.com

SKIING

The Sheffield Ski Village is the home of the UK's only half-pipe and offers visitors a good variety of artificial slopes. Snowboarding and skiing enthusiasts are well catered for and if you need a helping hand, there's plenty of tuition on offer, too. ⓐ 4 Vale Road ⓣ 0114 276 0044 ⓦ www.sheffieldskivillage.co.uk

FOOTBALL

If you're a football fan then look out for Sheffield Wednesday based in the Hillsborough Stadium, Sheffield United over on Bramall Lane and the Hallam Football Club located on Sandygate Road.

SWIMMING

The Ponds Forge International Sports Centre was built for the World Student Games in 1991 but there was plenty of forward planning involved, too. Today the public facilities include an Olympic-sized swimming pool, an array of diving boards, a

leisure pool with a wave machine and a lazy river. The large sports hall here is also used for major basketball events.
ⓐ Sheaf Street ⓣ 0114 223 3400 ⓦ www.ponds-forge.co.uk

SPA TIME

For an afternoon of relaxation and a spot of indulgence, the Belaqua Spa at the Mercure Sheffield St Paul's Hotel is your best bet in the city centre. In addition to the treatments on offer, here you'll also find a swimming pool, a sauna, a steam room and gym facilities. ⓐ 119 Norfolk Street ⓣ 0114 278 2000
ⓦ www.mercure.com

△ Take to the slopes at Sheffield Ski Village

Accommodation

Thanks to Sheffield's top five position in the list of Britain's biggest cities, there is a wide selection of hotels available to visitors. The choice is huge and accommodates all budgets – from the luxurious to the basic. The options are also spread out across the city and beyond, so whether you need a convenient stop just off the M1, a base in the very centre or a remote retreat not too far from the Peak District, the choice is yours.

VICTORIA QUAYS

Many of the inner city hotels can be found clustered around Victoria Quays. This quiet area, a short walk north of the city centre, is famous for the recently regenerated Sheffield and Tinsley canal, and many of the rooms here have great views over the water. Ⓝ Tram: Fitzalan Square/Ponds Forge

Ibis £ The Ibis is an affordable hotel that gets the job done. There are no bells and whistles but the rooms are comfortable, clean and kept up to date with features you'd expect from any major hotel chain. Wi-Fi is available and the staff are always friendly. Ⓐ Shude Hill Ⓣ 0114 241 9600 Ⓦ www.ibishotel.com Ⓝ Tram: Fitzalan Square/Ponds Forge

Holiday Inn Royal Victoria Sheffield ££ This Grade II listed building comes complete with a ballroom that doubles as a banquet hall, fitness facilities in the dance studio and the award-winning Cunningham's Restaurant. There's also a lounge set aside for quiet time where guests can sit back with a cup of

coffee and read without interruption. ⓐ Victoria Station Road
ⓣ 0114 276 8822 ⓦ www.holidayinnsheffield.co.uk
ⓝ Tram: Fitzalan Square/Ponds Forge

The Park Inn ££ The Park Inn might not look like much from the
outside but the interior is well finished and comfortable, the
high-speed internet connection is handy and the breakfast
is really rather good. The hotel is also next door to a very
affordable car park, and the city centre and train station are
only a five-minute walk away. ⓐ Blonk Street ⓣ 0114 220 4000
ⓦ www.sheffield.parkinn.co.uk ⓝ Tram: Fitzalan Square/
Ponds Forge

Hilton ££–£££ Occupying a prime quayside location, this red
brick building can legitimately claim to be one of the best hotels
in the city. The restaurant, café and bar serve up great views and
there are frequent fitness classes at the gym – to suit all
schedules. ⓐ Furnival Road ⓣ 0114 252 5500 ⓦ www.hilton.com
ⓝ Tram: Fitzalan Square/Ponds Forge

CITY CENTRE
Jurys Inn Sheffield ££ This is a popular spot with parents who
are scouting out Sheffield as a university option for their
children, and also with civil servants in town for work at the
nearby Department of Work and Pensions. It's in a great location
and you won't find better value for money in a more central area.
Walk out of the door and you're in the midst of all things Sheffield.
ⓐ 119 Eyre Street ⓣ 0114 291 2222 ⓦ www.jurysinns.com
ⓝ Tram: Sheffield Station/Sheffield Hallam University

Premier Inn Sheffield City Centre ££ Within easy striking distance of the Castle Square tram stop, this budget-friendly hotel is also handy for drivers, who can leave their cars at the nearby multi-storey car park on Arundel Gate. The hotel is a relatively new addition to this area and the modern rooms are well insulated against the background noise of the city centre. ⓐ Angel Street ① 0870 238 3324 ⓦ www.premierinn.com ⓝ Tram: Castle Square

The Leopold Hotel ££ This Grade II listed building has been transformed from an old grammar school into a four-star boutique hotel with membership of the Small Luxury Hotels of the World. The nearby Leopold Square is also a recent addition to the city, with a good selection of restaurants and bars, all a stone's throw from City Hall and the city's main shopping area. ⓐ Leopold Square ① 0114 252 4000 ⓦ www.leopoldhotel.co.uk ⓝ Tram: City Hall

Mercure Sheffield St Paul's Hotel ££-£££ Beyond the popular spa at this relatively new hotel, the four-star facilities here provide guests with all the modern conveniences and views over some splendid fountains and the Peace Gardens. The international flora and fauna of the indoor Winter Gardens are mere metres away and can be accessed without going outside. ⓐ 119 Norfolk Street ① 0114 278 2000 ⓦ www.mercure.com ⓝ Tram: Cathedral

OUT OF TOWN
The Beauchief £-££ If you head out of Sheffield in a southwesterly direction you encounter the parks and the Peak District, but before that there's the Beauchief. With four acres of private

gardens and only 50 rooms, it is ideal for some peace and quiet or a romantic getaway. The corridor linking the reception to the restaurant bridges a babbling brook, and the nearby historic village of Dore is a great day trip destination. ⓐ 161 Abbeydale Road South ⓣ 0114 262 0500 ⓦ www.beauchief-hotel.co.uk

Whitley Hall Hotel ££ This 16th-century mansion is a short drive out of the city but the surrounding countryside and grandeur are worth the trip. The luscious grounds are patrolled by peacocks, while the rooms boast a good mix of antiques and modern comforts. The open fireplaces, stone walls and chandeliers create a relaxed atmosphere and make the hall a popular spot for special occasions. ⓐ Elliott Lane ⓣ 0114 245 4444 ⓦ www.whitleyhall.com

🔺 *There are numerous hotels in the Victoria Quays area*

THE BEST OF SHEFFIELD

You'll never be short of something to do in Sheffield and if your itinerary doesn't include a lot of room to manoeuvre, then there are certain sights that are not to be missed.

TOP 10 ATTRACTIONS

- **The Peace Gardens** A popular spot full of flora, fountains and Sheffield citizens enjoying the great outdoors during their lunch break (see page 45).

- **Sheffield Cathedral** A true symbol of the city and an interesting mix of architectural styles spanning several centuries (see page 45).

- **The Millennium Gallery** and **The Winter Garden** Four incredibly diverse galleries attached to one of the world's largest and most impressive glasshouses (see pages 48 and 51).

- **Ponds Forge International Sports Centre** A great attraction for swimming enthusiasts with an Olympic-sized pool, diving boards and a lazy river (see page 20).

- **Ecclesall Road** A vibrant street full to the brim with cafés, bars, restaurants and one-of-a-kind shops (see page 57).

- **Weston Park Museum** One of the finest museums in Sheffield found in the well-kept grounds of Weston Park (see page 64).

- **The Crucible** Known internationally as the home of the World Snooker Championship and famous in its own right as one of the best theatres in the UK (see page 48).

- **Kelham Island Museum** A powerful and fascinating window on the history of Sheffield steel (see page 50).

- **Meadowhall Shopping Centre** Over 270 shops selling everything you need, come rain or shine (see page 73).

- **The Peak District** The first national park in Britain and a stunning landscape teeming with stone villages, right on your doorstep (see page 78).

The Peace Gardens

Suggested itineraries

The best itineraries to help you make the most of Sheffield, depending on how long you have in the city.

HALF-DAY: SHEFFIELD IN A HURRY

If your time is limited to a single morning or afternoon, then head straight to **Tudor Square**. Here you can enjoy the free art collections at the **Graves Gallery** above the library, the architectural delights of the **Lyceum** and the **Crucible theatres**, the thousands of plants in the **Winter Garden** and, just next door, the **Millennium Gallery**. If, however, you wish to focus on one thing, then make it the **Sheffield Art Collection** at the **Graves Gallery** and relax with a coffee at the café, just after gallery four.

1 DAY: TIME TO SEE A LITTLE MORE

After making the most of Tudor Square in the morning, exit the Winter Garden, pass through the **Peace Gardens** and head towards the shopping opportunities on **Fargate**. Make your way through **Orchard Square** and set aside some time for a spot of lunch in **Leopold Square** at one of its many restaurants. Afterwards, head along **West Street**, past the **City Hall**, towards the **Turner Museum of Glass** on Mappin Street. Continue walking west and you'll arrive at the **University of Sheffield** with its famous **Arts Tower** on Bolsover Street. Just beyond this, is **Weston Park** and the **Weston Park Museum**. To finish off your day, head back into the city centre and take in a show at the **Crucible**, the **Lyceum** or the **Studio**.

2–3 DAYS: SHORT CITY BREAK

Over two or three days you can easily explore the attractions of Tudor Square, make the most of West Street and have time left for some inner city sporting fun, not to mention the attractions found just outside the city centre. A morning in the swimming pools of the **Ponds Forge International Sports Centre** is great fun, as is an afternoon spent on the slopes at the **Sheffield Ski Village**. A short ride on the Supertram will take you to the **Centertainment** complex where you'll find restaurants, a cinema, a bowling alley and the **Meadowhall Retail Park**. Alternatively, stick to the shops in the centre and then take a stroll along Ecclesall Road – home to one-of-a-kind boutiques, cafés and fine dining restaurants.

🔺 *The Weston Park Museum has recently undergone a huge renovation*

Something for nothing

It's easy to see Sheffield without spending a penny, especially if you like a good stroll, so set aside a day and walk from one end of the city to the other. Start in the north, near the old marketplace and the industrial heritage along the canal, make your way through the gardens and galleries in the centre, and finish at the university in the west.

More often than not there will be a free festival or photo exhibition happening when you're in town so pop into the foyer of the library on **Surrey Street** and see what's advertised.

For a dose of the great outdoors there's a good selection of parks in Sheffield. In the west **Endcliffe Park** and **Weston Park** are a good choice, and in the centre slightly smaller pockets of green can be found around Surrey Street.

Sheffield is also a very photogenic city and there are many beautiful buildings and sculptures worthy of a snapshot. Keen photographers should start with the *Cutting Edge* sculpture at the train station, before heading into the city centre.

When it rains

There are many museums and galleries in Sheffield and, just as in London, the majority are free. With so many to choose from it can be difficult to pick one that that suits you, so it's always a good idea to plan ahead and minimise your exposure to the elements in the process. This website, listing every major museum and exhibition in Sheffield, is particularly useful for forward planners: ⓦ www.museums-sheffield.org.uk

The Supertram network is another handy resource when it comes to making the most of the city and staying dry. An unlimited day pass is inexpensive, and with it visitors can travel from the city centre to the cinema and the bowling alley at the **Centertainment** complex, and then onto the indoor **Meadowhall Shopping Centre**.

If museums and shopping don't appeal to you when it's raining, then you can take charge of just how wet you want to get with a swim at the Ponds Forge International Sports Centre. Alternatively ice-skating at Ice Sheffield is a great way to pass the time when the heavens open.

On arrival

Sheffield is easy to get around, no matter what mode of transport you use. It's straightforward to access the city by car and there are plenty of parking spaces. However, most people choose to arrive by train or tram, simply because the city's public transport system is so reliable and stress free. Furthermore, the trams and buses have access to areas of the city that cars don't and the ring road system can, on occasion, be a bit tricky. Large areas of the city centre are pedestrianised, so if you can get around on public transport you'll find it easier to get to where you want to go. If at any point you become disorientated then don't hesitate to ask for help. The people of Sheffield are very friendly and are more than happy to offer assistance.

ARRIVING
By air
The closest airport is Robin Hood Airport Doncaster Sheffield, approximately 25 miles east of the city. A dedicated shuttle bus connects the airport to Doncaster train station, and from here Sheffield city centre is only a 25-minute journey away on the Transpennine Express. Alternative train services also link Doncaster to Sheffield, although the journey times vary. Tickets can be purchased on the bus and on the train.

The airport opened in 2005 and is connected to a number of international destinations, including many of the European hubs. The building is modern and spacious but not big enough to get lost in. There are a few shops and cafés here, too, in what is essentially one terminal. Ⓦ www.robinhoodairport.com

By rail

Sheffield train station is connected to all the major cities in the UK and, after a multimillion pound refurbishment, this Derbyshire sandstone building is rather nice to travel through too. The station is located on the eastern edge of the city centre, a ten-minute walk away from all the main sights and attractions. Just outside of the station is Sheaf Square, a useful meeting point with a taxi rank, a waterfall and the stunning *Cutting Edge* sculpture.

The station itself is medium-sized with a bridge connecting the platforms. The ticket office is apparent the moment you enter the building and there are a number of coffee shops and magazine stands. The four-lane road between the station and the walk up to the city centre is particularly busy and there's no subway, so be sure to stick to the pedestrian crossing.

The station is by no means known as a hotspot for pickpockets; however, just as with any other busy public area, it's best to keep an eye on your wallet and your possessions.

By bus

Sheffield's primary bus station was also recently refurbished. This huge investment in the city's infrastructure was a key component in a regeneration initiative known as the Heart of the City Project. The result in this case is the Sheffield Interchange – an efficient design where dozens of buses and National Express coaches drop off and pick up passengers every hour.

The Sheffield Interchange can be found in Pond Square – opposite the train station and just off Harmer Lane and Pond

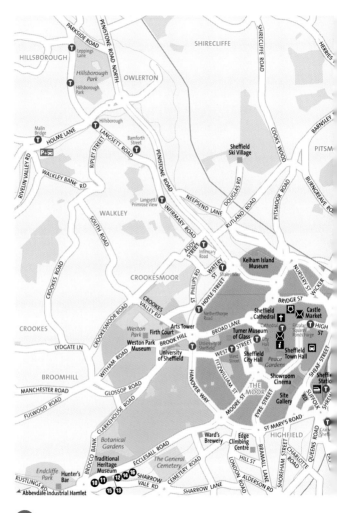

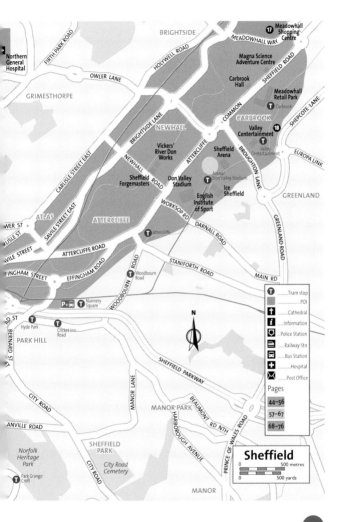

BRIGHTSIDE

Meadowhall Shopping Centre ⓱

MEADOWHALL WAY

Northern General Hospital

FIRTH PARK ROAD

HOLYWELL ROAD

Magna Science Adventure Centre

SHEFFIELD ROAD

OWLER LANE

Carbrook Hall

GRIMESTHORPE

BRIGHTSIDE LANE

COMMON

Meadowhall Retail Park

Ⓣ Carbrook

NEWHALL

CARBROOK ⓲

Valley Centertainment

SHEPCOTE LANE

Vickers' River Don Works

ATTERCLIFFE

Ⓣ Valley Centertainment

EUROPA LINK

CARLISLE STREET EAST

NEWHALL

Sheffield Arena

BROUGHTON LANE

Sheffield Forgemasters

ROAD

Don Valley Stadium

Arena/ Don Valley Stadium

GREENLAND

SAVILE STREET EAST

WER ST

ATLAS

ATTERCLIFFE

WORKSOP RD

English Institute of Sport

Ice Sheffield

GREENLAND ROAD

RUSLE STREET

Ⓣ Attercliffe

DARNALL ROAD

NVILLE STREET

ATTERCLIFFE ROAD

STANIFORTH ROAD

MAIN RD

FINGHAM STREET

EFFINGHAM ROAD

WOODBOURN ROAD

Ⓣ Woodbourn Road

P+🚌 Nunnery Square

N

BERNARD ST

O ST

Ⓣ Hyde Park

Ⓣ Cricket Inn Road

PARK HILL

SHEFFIELD PARKWAY

MANOR LANE

BEAUMONT RD NTH

PRINCE OF WALES ROAD

CITY ROAD

MANOR PARK

HARBOROUGH AVENUE

ANVILLE ROAD

SHEFFIELD PARK

Norfolk Heritage Park

City Road Cemetery

CITY ROAD

MANOR

Ⓣ Park Grange Croft

Ⓣ	........Tram stop
	POI
✝	........Cathedral
🛈	........Information
🅟	........Police Station
🚃	........Railway Stn
🚌	........Bus Station
✚	........Hospital
✉	........Post Office

Pages
44–56
57–67
68–76

Sheffield
0 ___ 500 metres
0 ___ 500 yards

Street. If you are approaching the interchange from the city centre a useful landmark to help you get there is the O2 Academy Sheffield on Arundel Gate. The interchange is directly behind this venue, which is itself next to the Arundel Gate car park and just over the road from the Crucible theatre.

The nearest tram stop to the bus station is Fitzalan Square/Ponds Forge on Commercial Street, just before this stretch of road turns into the High Street. All trams stop at this station at some point on their route. From this stop the Sheffield Interchange is short walk down Fitzalan, which turns into Flat Street, which then turns into Pond Street. The route is also signposted.

The Free Bee bus, which circles the city centre, departs from the Sheffield Interchange. From the interchange, the bus stops at Flat Street, Castle Street, Arundel Gate, Norfolk Street, the Town Hall, Furnival Gate, Charter Row, Fitzwilliam Gate, Eyre Street, Furnival Street and the train station, before returning to the interchange.

Unlike the National Express service, the Megabus routes across the United Kingdom do not use the Sheffield Interchange so if this is part of your plan to get into or out of Sheffield, you need to be at the Meadowhall Shopping Centre transport interchange. This is linked to the city centre Sheffield Interchange by local buses and the Supertram.

By tram

Sheffield's Supertram is very easy to navigate, but the lines do cross over at certain points. Simply imagine three lines that intersect in the city centre and spread out to cover the far-flung

🔺 *Sheaf Square and the limestone façade of the station*

suburbs in the northeast, the northwest and the southeast segments of the city.

The yellow route begins at a station called Stocksbridge, northwest of the city centre and close to Sheffield Wednesday's Hillsborough Stadium. The route runs down into the city centre, along West Street and out to the northeast, passing the stadiums and ice rinks of Attercliffe and Carbrook, before terminating at the Meadowhall Interchange.

The blue route begins slightly west of Hillsborough at Malin Bridge in the northwest and follows route one into the city centre, before splitting off at the Fitzalan Square/Ponds Forge station. From here this branch goes all the way to the network's most southeastern stop – Halfway.

The purple route begins in the city centre at the Cathedral and covers a smaller portion of route two in addition to a small offshoot at the very end of the line. The last station at the south end of this branch is called Herdings Park. Herdings Park and the stop just before it, Herdings/Leighton Road, are the only stations not accessible on route two.

The most economical way to get around the Supertram network is to use a Day Rider ticket. This travel pass allows you unlimited access to the entire network for a day. Free route maps are available from the tourism office on Norfolk Row.

By car

Sheffield is well suited for cars and pedestrians alike, but the city centre is generally the domain of the latter. When approaching the city on the M1 drivers can exit at Junction 33 or Junction 34. Junction 33 leads onto the high speed Parkway which terminates

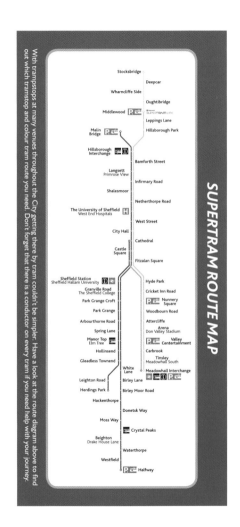

With tramstops at many venues throughout the City getting there by tram couldn't be simpler. Have a look at the route diagram above to find out which tramstop and colour tram route you need. Don't forget that there is a conductor on every tram if you need help with your journey.

SUPERTRAM ROUTE MAP

Stocksbridge

Deepcar

Wharncliffe Side

Oughtibridge

Middlewood P 🚏

SUPERTRAMLINK

Leppings Lane

Malin Bridge P 🚏

Hillsborough Park

Hillsborough Interchange 🚌 🚆

Bamforth Street

Langsett
Primrose View

Infirmary Road

Shalesmoor

Netherthorpe Road

The University of Sheffield
West End Hospitals H

West Street

City Hall

Cathedral

Castle Square

Fitzalan Square

Sheffield Station
Sheffield Hallam University 🚆 🚌

Hyde Park

Granville Road
The Sheffield College

Cricket Inn Road

P 🚏 Nunnery Square

Park Grange Croft

Woodbourn Road

Park Grange

Attercliffe

Arbourthorne Road

Arena
Don Valley Stadium

Spring Lane

P 🚏 Valley Centertainment

Manor Top 🚌
Elm Tree

Carbrook

Hollinsend

Tinsley
Meadowhall South

Gleadless Townend

White Lane

Meadowhall Interchange
🚌 🚆 🚍 P 🚏

Leighton Road

Birley Lane

Herdings Park

Birley Moor Road

Hackenthorpe

Donetsk Way

Moss Way

🚌 Crystal Peaks

Beighton
Drake House Lane

Waterthorpe

Westfield

P 🚏 Halfway

at the Park Square Roundabout, in close proximity to the hotel district and the Ponds Forge International Sports Centre. Junction 34 on the other hand is located next to the Meadowhall Shopping Centre. This exit is a good idea for drivers who wish to make the most of the park-and-ride Supertram scheme.

FINDING YOUR FEET

It isn't too hard to find your way around the centre of Sheffield, but it is a good idea to take a detailed map with you when you venture out into the Ecclesall Road, Attercliffe and Carbrook areas. There isn't a lot of crime in the city, but it is advisable to be aware of your personal belongings in crowded places.

ORIENTATION

To get your bearings in the city centre remember that the canal and the cathedral are to the north, the train station and bus interchange are to the east, the Peace Gardens and The Moor are to the south, and the City Hall and the University of Sheffield are to the west. Ecclesall Road lies to the southwest of the centre and Meadowhall to the northeast.

GETTING AROUND

The centre of Sheffield is easy to get around on foot; however, for everything else the Supertram really is super! The network gives you access to all the main sites and it's very affordable. Alternatively, taxi fares aren't too expensive and you can easily find taxi ranks dotted around the city.

◗ *Sheffield City Hall*

 THE CITY OF
Sheffield

Introduction to city areas

The city of Sheffield is spread out over approximately 225 sq km (140 sq miles). Within the city boundaries there are three key areas that all visitors should take the time to explore. Each area has a lot to offer and adds something special to the character of the city.

Looking at Sheffield from above, most of the **city centre** is contained within the circular A61 road. It's in this area that you'll find the highest concentration of galleries, theatres, cafés, shops and museums, not to mention a good deal of green space.

Southwest of the city centre, **Ecclesall Road** is brimming with shops, bars, parks, museums and university students. The pace of life here is a little less hectic than in the centre, and the parks help maintain a laid-back and easy-going vibe.

In the great industrial days of yesteryear, **Attercliffe** and **Carbrook** were dominated by the Sheffield steelworks, but today it's the domain of sport stadiums, music arenas, ice rinks, the English Institute of Sport and a fair few shops.

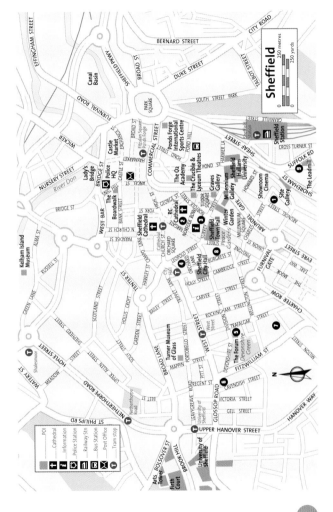

The city centre

A large number of Sheffield's most popular attractions can be found in the city centre, between the boundaries of the canal to the north and Bramall Lane to the south. Of particular interest are the many beautiful 19th-century buildings and squares – preserved, restored and enhanced as part of the £130 million Heart of the City Project. Prime examples include the Lyceum Theatre, Tudor Square, the train station and the Peace Gardens. The city centre is also home to some of the best shops around, intimate cafés, renowned restaurants, more than half of the city's live music venues and the majority of Sheffield's internationally acclaimed theatres and museums.

SIGHTS & ATTRACTIONS

The Canal Basin
The Sheffield Canal revolutionised the city's industries when it opened in 1819, connecting Sheffield to Tinsley and the river Don. Today, however, the coal barges and steel shipments have been replaced with pleasure cruisers and waterside cafés. The basin was renamed Victoria Quays in 1994 and attractions include Sheaf Quay and the Cobweb Bridge, suspended beneath the old railway viaduct. Ⓝ Tram: Fitzalan Square/Ponds Forge

City Hall and the War Memorial
The City Hall opened in 1932 and, if you look closely at the columns, you can still see the damage inflicted when a World War II bomb detonated nearby. The War Memorial is just in front

of the hall and features a bronze base and four sculptured soldiers, bowing their heads. This was unveiled in 1925 to honour the 5,000 men from Sheffield who died in World War I.
ⓐ Barker's Pool ☎ 0114 223 3740 ⓦ www.sheffieldcityhall.co.uk
Ⓝ Tram: City Hall

The Peace Gardens

The Peace Gardens occupy the site where St Paul's Church once stood. The name can be traced back to the anticipation of peace in Europe following Germany's signing of the 1938 Munich Agreement. Even though this agreement didn't succeed in appeasing the Nazis, the name stuck and was formally adopted in 1985. The gardens were redesigned in 1997 and today include fountains, waterways, beautiful bronze statues and lawns.
Ⓝ Tram: Cathedral

Sheaf Square and the *Cutting Edge* Sculpture

There's no better introduction to the city of Sheffield than Sheaf Square. This approach to the train station includes an array of cascading waterfalls, fountains, a public square and its *Cutting Edge* sculpture. The 60-tonne artwork is made of stainless steel produced in Sheffield and pays tribute to the city's industrial achievements. It's best seen at night when the two ends of this 90 m long structure glow red and blue.
Ⓝ Tram: Sheffield Station/Sheffield Hallam University

Sheffield Cathedral

The cathedral is an interesting mishmash of architectural styles, reflecting various additions to the building since construction began in the fifteenth century. Of particular interest inside is the tomb of George Talbot, sixth Earl of Shrewsbury and long-term jailer of Mary, Queen of Scots. ➌ Church Street ☎ 0114 275 3434 ⓦ www.sheffield-cathedral.co.uk 🕒 08.30–17.00 Mon & Tues, 08.30–18.30 Wed–Fri, 09.45–15.30 Sat, 07.45–19.30 Sun Ⓝ Tram: Cathedral

Town Hall

The Town Hall was opened by Queen Victoria in 1897 and designed by E W Mountford, the winner of a city council competition to find the best architect for the job. A statue of the Roman god Vulcan dominates the top of the tallest tower, representing Sheffield's steel industry, in addition to the collection of living, botanical sculptures at the front that depict steel workers carrying out their tasks. Free 45-minute tours of this Grade I listed building are available, but it's necessary to book in advance. ➌ Pinstone Street ☎ 0114 272 6444 ⓦ www.sheffield.gov.uk Ⓝ Tram: Cathedral

Tudor Square

This is a great spot to get your bearings in Sheffield and, following a huge redesign at the beginning of 2010, it's very picturesques too. From this square you can access the Lyceum Theatre, the Crucible, the City Library, the Graves Gallery, the Winter Garden and the Millennium Gallery. There are also benches dotted around, making Tudor Square perfect for people watching. Ⓝ Tram: Castle Square

◔ *Inside the Winter Garden*

The Winter Garden

This structure is one of the biggest modern glasshouses in Europe and was opened by the Queen in 2003. Inside, visitors can enjoy more than 2,000 plants from the farthest reaches of the planet kept at a constant temperature, making this a pleasant escape all year round. Other highlights include the kinetic water sculpture by Pete Rogers. ⓐ 90 Surrey Street ⓣ 0114 221 1900 ⓗ 08.00–23.00 Mon–Sat, 08.00–20.00 Sun ⓝ Tram: Castle Square

CULTURE

The Boardwalk

At the forefront of live music in Sheffield for over 50 years, you might have heard of some of the acts who've performed here: they include the Sex Pistols, Genesis and The Clash – who made their debut on this very stage. ⓐ Snig Hill ⓣ 0114 279 9090 ⓦ www.theboardwalklive.co.uk ⓝ Tram: Castle Square

City Hall

This venue attracts everyone from Jools Holland to Status Quo, and it's also a well-known spot for classical acts, including the BBC Philharmonic who return here annually for the Sheffield International Concert Season. ⓐ Barker's Pool ⓣ 0114 278 9789 ⓦ www.sheffieldcityhall.co.uk ⓝ Tram: City Hall

The Crucible

Nothing sums up Sheffield quite like the Crucible – the theatrical powerhouse of South Yorkshire and home of the

World Snooker Championship. After a £15 million refurbishment, the theatre re-opened in 2009 with an ambitious production schedule to follow on from legendary past performances, including Chekhov's *Swan Song* starring Sir Ian McKellen. The thrust stage, extending into the auditorium, ensures that none of the 980 seats are more than 22 m from the performers. The Crucible also houses a smaller performance space called the Studio. **a** 55 Norfolk Street **t** 0114 249 6000 **w** www.sheffieldtheatres.co.uk **e** info@sheffieldtheatres.co.uk **n** Tram: Castle Square

△ *The world-famous Crucible Theatre*

Graves Gallery

This art gallery on the top floor of the Central Library is named after Dr J G Graves, who helped fund the construction of this Art Deco building and contributed to its permanent collections. There are seven exhibition rooms housing pieces by Cézanne and Turner, as well as more contemporary works by artists such as Sam Taylor-Wood. Free audio guides are available at reception. Surrey Street 0114 278 2600 www.museums-sheffield.org.uk 10.00–16.00 Mon–Fri, 10.00–17.00 Sat, closed Sun Tram: Castle Square

Kelham Island Museum

Built on a 900-year-old man-made island and formerly an electricity generating station, this museum provides a fascinating insight into Sheffield's industrial past. Alma Street 0114 272 2106 www.simt.co.uk ask@simt.co.uk 10.00–16.00 Mon–Thur, 11.00–16.45 Sun, closed Fri & Sat Tram: Shalesmoor Admission charge

The Lyceum

The Lyceum is more than just the home of pantomime in Sheffield. After a £12 million restoration programme the theatre re-opened in 1990, revealing painstakingly restored sculpted cherubs and frescoes. Today the Lyceum is the primary South Yorkshire stop for the touring shows of London's West End. 55 Norfolk Street 0114 249 6000 www.sheffieldtheatres.co.uk info@sheffieldtheatres.co.uk Tram: Castle Square

The Millennium Gallery

Inside this building the Ruskin, Craft and Design, Metalwork and Special Exhibition Galleries showcase local and travelling art, including pieces from the Tate galleries. The Metalwork Gallery is particularly interesting and traces the history of the city's steel industry back to a time when Sheffield produced 90 per cent of the steel used in Great Britain and 50 per cent of that used in Europe. ⓐ Arundel Gate ⓣ 0114 278 2600 ⓦ www.museums-sheffield.org.uk ⓒ 10.00–17.00 Mon–Sat, 11.00–17.00 Sun ⓝ Tram: Castle Square

The O₂ Academy Sheffield

Opened by local hero Jarvis Cocker in 2008, the academy hosts big acts and emerging talent in its two auditoriums. The whole venue is standing only. ⓐ 37–43 Arundel Gate ⓣ 0844 477 2000 ⓦ www.o2academysheffield.co.uk ⓝ Tram: Castle Square

⬥ The Millennium Gallery

The Showroom Cinema

More than just a cinema, the Showroom houses film festivals, the Workstation creative arts business centre, a café that does a superb Sunday lunch and a bar frequented by Sheffield's glitterati. The annual Sheffield Doc/Fest, the Sensoria Festival of Music and Film, and the Sheffield Adventure Film Festival are all held here. ⓐ 7 Paternoster Row ⓣ 0114 276 3534 ⓦ www.showroomworkstation.org.uk ⓝ Tram: Sheffield Station/ Sheffield Hallam University

Site Gallery

This gallery supports artists just beginning their creative careers and, with endorsements from Pulp front man Jarvis Cocker, it attracts the top talent from across the world. The many exhibitions are complemented by opportunities to meet the artists and the gallery is well known for its sculptors, jewellers and silversmiths. ⓐ Brown Street ⓣ 0114 281 2077 ⓦ www.sitegallery.org ⓔ info@sitegallery.org ⓛ 11.00–17.30 Tues–Sat, closed Sun & Mon ⓝ Tram: Sheffield Station/Sheffield Hallam University

RETAIL THERAPY

High Street shopping

You can find all of the big high street brands in the centre of Sheffield, with the majority located on **Fargate**, a pedestrianised shopping strip in the heart of the city. Fargate stretches from the **Barker's Pool** market area up to the High Street, just next to the Cathedral. An alleyway away from

Fargate is the **Orchard Square Shopping Centre**, a pleasant courtyard lined with cafés, clothes shops, a large bookshop and local jewellery makers.

Slightly west of Fargate is **Division Street** where shoppers will find designer stores including Eton – a women's boutique with clothes fresh from the catwalk. Another popular spot on Division Street is **The Forum** – an indoor hub of independent shops selling everything from Dr Martens to scented candles the size of your head.

When walking along Division Street towards the city centre, it's worth taking a left at the crossroads with **Carver Street**. Here you'll find the finest fashion from the 60s and the 70s at **Freshman's Vintage Clothes**, including flares, fitted leather jackets and fluorescent green chiffon shirts!

⬣ *The Wheel of Sheffield outside the Town Hall on Fargate*

Markets

In the **Barker's Pool** area just outside the City Hall, you'll often find travelling **farmers' markets**. The markets normally appear on the last weekend of the month, however the schedules vary – particularly at Christmas when the European markets arrive, selling delicious treats from the continent.

Castle Market or, as it's simply known, the **Market** is a permanent collection of greengrocers, fishmongers and local butchers north of the High Street. This indoor collection of stalls was built on the remains of **Sheffield Castle** and there's been a market on this spot since the late-13th century. Today, however, there are plans to move the traders to a new, purpose-built development on **The Moor**, south of the city centre.

TAKING A BREAK

Fusion Organic Café £ ❶ Housed in the restored Butchers Works (a former cutlery makers), this charming café serves homemade cakes, every kind of coffee imaginable and a spoonful of heritage. ⓐ 72 Arundel Street ❶ 0114 252 5974 ⓦ www.academyofmakers.co.uk ❶ 09.00–16.30 Mon–Fri, 10.00–15.30 Sat, closed Sun

22A Norfolk Row £–££ ❷ This family-run tearoom is an essential stop on any trip. Customers are welcomed with an aroma of freshly baked goodies at the front and a restaurant, serving more substantial fare, at the rear. ⓐ 22A Norfolk Row ❶ 0114 276 7462 ❶ 08.00–17.00 Mon–Sat, closed Sun

Mama's and Leonies ££ ❸ A popular Italian restaurant whose proud owners boast that they out-cook every other pizzeria in the city – the Pizza Papa here is heavenly. ⓐ 111–115 Norfolk St ⓣ 0114 272 0490 ⓦ www.mamas.co.uk ⓛ 09.00–23.00 Mon–Thur, 09.30–23.30 Fri & Sat, closed Sun

AFTER DARK

BARS

Sheffield isn't short of a bar or two, so it's a good idea to plan a night out based around the areas that match your mood. West Street, for example, mixes traditional Yorkshire pubs with student hotspots, Leopold Square offers a distinct piano-bar cocktail culture and Tudor Square caters to theatre lovers.

Cubana ❹ To get an idea of what Cubana's all about, imagine the best tapas in Sheffield, lots of Latin music, a cocktail list as long as your arm and free salsa classes. This bar also sells real Cuban cigars, hosts live music every week and is the preferred performance spot when the Buena Vista Social Club come to town. ⓐ 34 Trippet Lane ⓣ 0114 276 0475 ⓦ www.cubanatapasbar.co.uk ⓛ 17.00–01.00 Mon–Fri, 12.00–01.00 Sat, closed Sun

The Forum Café and Bar ❺ This shopping hub is also home to a great little bar, known for its extended happy hours and entertainment ranging from club nights to stand-up comedy. ⓐ Devonshire Street ⓣ 0114 272 0569

Ⓦ www.forumsheffield.co.uk Ⓛ 10.00–01.00 Mon–Thur, 10.00–02.00 Fri & Sat, 11.00–01.00 Sun

West One ❻ This relatively new courtyard collection of bars offers a varied choice of watering holes but Bar 360° is always a top spot. It's good for champagne cocktails and the crowd is a nice mix, too. Ⓐ 15 Fitzwilliam St Ⓣ 0114 276 6854 Ⓛ 16.00–24.00 Wed & Thur, 10.00–24.00 Fri & Sat, 16.00–24.00 Sun, closed Mon & Tues

NIGHTCLUBS

Corporation ❼ Known to many simply as 'the Corp', this club is one of the best in the country and it's got the accreditations from *Kerrang!* to back it up. Ⓐ Trafalgar Court, 2 Milton Street Ⓣ 0114 276 0262 Ⓦ www.corporation.org.uk Ⓔ mrkeef@corporation.org.uk

Embrace ❽ Imagine one giant glitter ball, five rooms and an Art Deco theme throughout, and you have an idea of what to expect from Embrace. Ⓐ 1 Burgress Street Ⓣ 0114 278 8811 Ⓦ www.embracenightclub.com Ⓔ Info@embracenightclub.com

The Leadmill ❾ Part nightclub, part live music venue, The Leadmill is the stuff of legend on the Sheffield music scene and clubbers come from miles around to soak up the atmosphere. Ⓐ 7 Leadmill Road Ⓣ 0114 221 2828 Ⓦ www.leadmill.co.uk Ⓔ information@leadmill.co.uk

Ecclesall Road & the university district

Ecclesall Road and the University of Sheffield are a short walk west from the city centre. This is an important area of the city and is home to many historical landmarks, scores of parks, a thriving micro-economy of independent shops and, of course, one of the best universities in the United Kingdom. The cultural pickings are rich, too, and include everything from the Hunter's Bar toll point to society retrospectives at the Weston Park Museum. As for the local cuisine, the restaurants here include a number of high-class eateries and one-off cafés. Throw in a generous spattering of boutique shops and a vibrant student scene, and you begin to see just what this wonderfully diverse area has to offer. Ecclesall Road can be easily reached on foot from the city centre, by jumping on buses 81, 82 or 86 from Leopold Street, or by taking the Supertram to its University of Sheffield stop.

SIGHTS AND ATTRACTIONS

Sheffield is known as Yorkshire's greenest city because of the many parks and woodlands within the city limits. Nearly a dozen of these are linked to Ecclesall Road and prime examples, such as **Ecclesall Wood** and **Endcliffe Park**, hide countless gems just waiting to be discovered. The buildings in this particularly affluent district of Sheffield are also an attraction in their own right, and you won't go far without catching sight of a grand manor house or an old abbey. A good starting point for any

explorer in this area is a wander along Ecclesall Road itself –
from the **Hunter's Bar** Roundabout at one end to the Moore
Street Roundabout at the other.

Endcliffe Park

This peaceful collection of duck ponds, babbling brooks and
monuments celebrating the Golden Jubilee of Queen Victoria
is just next to Hunter's Bar. The café in the park is a nice spot
for a zesty lemonade in the summer, and you'll often find a
circus or travelling fair in the open area at the centre. While
you're here it's worth visiting the Endcliffe Park Lodge, where
you'll encounter a particularly cheerful bunch of park rangers
who go out of their way to help visitors with information about
the nature trails and bike rides that run through the park.

Hunter's Bar

In the early 19th century, a toll bar was established on land
owned by the Hunter family, and it was here that travellers
passing in and out of the Peak District had to pay a fee. As far as
stone posts and wooden gates go it's a well-known landmark,
especially after local band Arctic Monkeys referred to it in their
song 'Fake Tales of San Francisco'.

Sheffield Botanical Gardens

Dating back to 1836, the Sheffield Botanical Gardens are home
to plants collected from all over the world as well as Grade II
listed glass pavilions. There's also an old bear pit here, but today
it's home to nothing more dangerous than creeping ivy. The
7.6 hectares (19 acres) of landscaped gardens here bear the

signature design trademarks of Robert Marnock, namely long winding paths and shrubs scattered among tree-strewn hills.
🅐 Clarkehouse Road 📞 0114 268 6001 🌐 www.sbg.org.uk
🕐 08.00–16.00 Mon–Fri, 10.00–16.00 Sat & Sun (winter); 08.00–19.45 Mon–Fri, 10.00–19.45 Sat & Sun (summer)

Sheffield General Cemetery

A cemetery might sound like an unusual attraction but this one has many interesting tales to tell. Opened in 1836, this Victorian burial ground is the site of around 87,700 graves. Interesting architecture here includes the Grade II listed Egyptian Gates, several tiers of catacombs and a monument to Mark Firth, Sheffield's most famous steel master. Free 90-minute tours run

🔺 *The restored glass pavilions of the Botanical Gardens*

The Gothic red brick and stone of Firth Court

on the first Sunday of every month at 14.00 from the gatehouse.
ⓐ Cemetery Road ⓦ www.gencem.org

The University of Sheffield

There are several buildings that Sheffielders identify with the
university, but it's Firth Court and the Arts Tower that really rule
the roost. The unmistakable red brick buildings of Firth Court
hide a tranquil courtyard and weekend visitors will often hear
an orchestra or quartet practising just out of sight. Be sure to
look out for the list of Nobel Peace Prize winners in the foyer
here, too. In comparison, the high-rise Arts Tower is a completely
different animal, and its many windows are used to display
complex and colourful artworks to passers-by. ⓐ Western Bank
ⓣ 0114 222 1299 ⓦ www.sheffield.ac.uk

Ward's Brewery

They stopped brewing here in 1999 after 159 years of production,
but as a tribute to the many famed ales that began life here, the
central tower of the old brewery has been incorporated into the
apartment complex now occupying the site. You can still buy
Ward's Best Bitter – the most famous ale to come out of this
brewery – but it's made elsewhere. ⓐ Ecclesall Road

Weston Park

The grounds of Weston Hall became Weston Park when
the city council bought the land and the hall for £15,750
in 1873. Robert Marnock was charged with transforming the
land into a pleasant public space and, since it opened on
6 September 1875, visitors have enjoyed the splendid

bandstand, the lake, the cherry blossoms and the Weston Park Museum. There are a number of interesting memorials here, too, and a weather station dating back to the 19th century.

CULTURE

Abbeydale Industrial Hamlet

In its heyday, this was one of the largest water-powered tool producers for miles around, and it was here that the power of the River Sheaf was harnessed to make everything from scythes to hay knives. Today the waterwheel process is on show for all to see at the Grade I listed site surrounded by the Ecclesall Woods. There's also a Boring Shop – not an especially dull place – but a building where holes were drilled into scythes. ⓐ Abbeydale Road South. To reach the Abbeydale Industrial Hamlet from Sheffield city centre, catch a bus from the High Street straight to the site. The journey takes approximately 20 minutes. ⓣ 0114 236 7731 ⓦ www.simt.co.uk ⓔ ask@simt.co.uk ⓛ 10.00–16.00 Mon–Thur, 11.00–16.45 Sun, closed Fri & Sat (Apr–Oct), closed Nov–Mar ⓝ Bus: 97 or 98

Traditional Heritage Museum

This independent museum, run by volunteers, features exhibitions all about local trades, crafts and occupations in Sheffield during the 19th and 20th centuries. There are several old shop fronts on display, providing a rare insight into what fuelled the area's economy in times gone by. It's also known as 'Sheffield's Secret Museum' as it's only open on certain

⬥ *Abbeydale Industrial Hamlet is a scheduled ancient monument*

days – namely the last Saturday of each month and Bank Holiday Mondays. ⓐ 605 Ecclesall Road ⓣ 0114 268 1270 ⓦ thm.group.shef.ac.uk ⓘ Admission charge

Weston Park Museum

After an extensive restoration in 2006, the Weston Park Museum is now a cutting edge repository of travelling exhibitions and permanent reflections on the life and times of Sheffield. The galleries within this grand old house – originally known as Weston Hall – contain information on everything from the devastating Sheffield Blitz in December 1940 to the fossilised bones of ancient, giant ground sloths. The City of Spirit room is especially evocative. ⓐ Western Bank ⓣ 0114 278 2600 ⓦ www.sheffieldgalleries.org.uk ⓛ 10.00–17.00 Mon–Sat, 11.00–17.00 Sun

RETAIL THERAPY

The majority of the shops in this area can be found on **Ecclesall Road** and the parallel-running **Sharrow Vale Road**. Many of these are one of a kind and you'll be hard pushed to find a big chain store anywhere around here.

Design Studio This kitsch shop sells everything from cow ornaments posing in red stiletto heels to one-off picture frames. You can easily spend hours in Design Studio entertaining yourself with its less-than-ordinary inventory. ⓐ 417–419 Ecclesall Road ⓣ 0114 268 3033 ⓛ 09.30–18.00 Mon–Sat, 12.00–17.00 Sun

The Famous Sheffield Shop This is a Sheffield institution, having traded nothing but the finest products made in Sheffield for over 25 years. The shelves are packed with a collection of carefully sourced books on the area that's second to none, and the proprietor is a true authority on the city. From trinket boxes and photo frames to hunting knives and pewter tankards, you'll find it here. 🅰 475 Ecclesall Road 🕐 0114 268 5701 🅦 www.sheffield-made.com 🅔 sales@sheffield-made.com 🕒 09.30–17.30 Mon–Fri, 09.00–17.30 Sat, closed Sun

Rio A very pleasant and elegantly decorated little shop that wouldn't look out of place on Rodeo Drive in Los Angeles. The high-end fashions on the rails here are exclusively for women, and it's just next door to the lovely Brookhouse Florist. 🅰 396–398 Sharrow Vale Road 🕐 0114 266 0106 🕒 10.00–17.30, Mon–Sat, closed Sun

TAKING A BREAK

Café Ceres £ ⑩ An authentic French café, expertly run by owners Jean-Paul and Caroline Strappazzo. The chickpea pâté and hummus whipped up here are especially tasty. 🅰 390 Sharrow Vale Road 🕐 0114 267 9090 🅦 www.cafeceres.com 🅔 info@cafeceres.com 🕒 09.15–16.30 Mon–Wed, 09.15–20.00 Thur–Sat, closed Sun & Bank Holidays

Fancie £ ⑪ This spectacular cake shop is the creation of Amanda Perry, who counts Professor Stephen Hawking as a fan of her baking! The cupcakes are heavenly and the aroma is enough to discourage you from ever leaving. ⓐ 388 Sharrow Vale Road ⓣ 0114 266 7238 ⓛ 10.00–18.00 Mon–Sat, 10.00–16.00 Sun

Nonna's ££–£££ ⓬ This café, restaurant, deli and wine bar really does deserve the many awards it has won. It's also a popular spot on the local nightlife circuit, but people really come here for the mouthwatering Italian cuisine. ⓐ 535–541 Ecclesall Road ⓣ 0114 268 6166 ⓦ www.nonnas.co.uk ⓔ info@nonnas.co.uk ⓛ breakfast 08.30–11.00 Mon–Sat, lunch 12.00–15.30 daily, dinner 18.00–21.30 Mon–Thur, 18.00–22.00 Fri & Sat, all-day menu 10.00–20.45 Sun

Walnut Live £££ ⓭ The cocktail bar at this venue is out of this world and one bite from any dish on the menu will hint at its

△ *Cake mecca*

Michelin-star aspirations. The menu is a mix of classic dishes with exciting new twists. ⓐ 557 Ecclesall Road ⓣ 0114 267 6566 ⓦ www.thewalnutclub.com ⓛ 12.00–23.00 Wed & Thur, 12.00–00.30 Fri–Sun, closed Mon & Tues

AFTER DARK

Beyond the exceptional bars attached to the restaurants at Nonna's and Walnut Live, there's an incredible selection of nightspots to explore on and around Ecclesall Road.

Abuelo ⓮ A Mexican-style bar that's great for a drink. There are no gimmicks here – just refreshing cocktails, fresh ingredients and barmen who know how to mix a mean mojito. ⓐ 543 Ecclesall Road ⓣ 0114 266 9221 ⓦ www.abuelo.co.uk ⓔ abuelosheffield@mac.com ⓛ 17.00–01.00 Sun & Mon, 12.00–01.00 Sat

The Lescar ⓯ A brilliant venue providing customers with a variety of top notch comedy, quizzes, live music and a great selection of ales. It's a chilled out spot with a varied clientele and a decent pub menu. ⓐ 303 Sharrow Vale Road ⓣ 0114 266 8974 ⓦ www.thelescarhuntersbar.co.uk ⓛ 12.00–24.00 Sun–Thur, 12.00–01.00 Fri & Sat

Porter Brook ⓰ A friendly and traditional local pub where you can have a proper conversation in comfortable surroundings. ⓐ 565 Ecclesall Road ⓣ 0114 266 5765 ⓛ 11.00–23.00 Mon–Sat, 12.00–23.00 Sun

Attercliffe & Carbrook

Sandwiched between the northernmost part of the city centre and the Meadowhall Shopping Centre, Attercliffe and Carbrook are full of attractions that you wouldn't, at first glance, expect to find here. The two areas are dominated by buildings constructed for a long gone industrial age, and from above you can see how this part of the city follows the route of the River Don – a telltale sign of the steel industry that once thrived on the abundant water power available here. Of the buildings that remain, the Vickers' River Don Works are some of the most impressive, giving visitors an idea of the scale involved when it came to manufacturing essential steel armaments for the British armed forces during World War II.

All of the steel mills, with the exception of Sheffield Forgemasters, have now closed and today Attercliffe and Carbrook are home to a number of large entertainment stadiums, Olympic-sized ice rinks, equally large retail parks, the Magna Science Adventure Centre and a fair amount of treasured heritage, including Carbrook Hall. This area of Sheffield has been through a fair amount, suffering first in the aftermath of World War II – when houses were cleared and not rebuilt, forcing many to leave – and then again with the decline of the steel industry in the 1980s. Today, however, it's thriving once again and represents a side to Sheffield that you just won't find in the city centre, or out towards Ecclesall Road and the west.

SIGHTS & ATTRACTIONS

Carbrook Hall

This building has seen many owners in its 900-year history, and an equally high number of cosmetic alterations. The oldest surviving part – a wing added in the seventeenth century – is protected as a Grade II listed building, while tales linking Carbrook Hall to the English Civil War help perpetuate its reputation as one of the most haunted houses in Sheffield. These days a pub, it is worth popping in for a pint and the ghoulish tale of Colonel John Bright, a loyal soldier in Oliver Cromwell's army. ⓐ 537 Attercliffe Common ⓣ 0114 244 0117 ⓦ www.carbrookhall.co.uk ⓛ 12.00–23.00 Mon–Thur, 12.00–23.30 Fri & Sat, 12.00–22.45 Sun ⓝ Tram: Carbrook

The English Institute of Sport

A key component in the Olympic aspirations of the UK's elite athletes, the state-of-the-art facilities here are also open to the public for fencing, martial arts, coached sports and more. It's possible to arrange individual guided tours of the facilities, by phoning ahead and paying a small fee. ⓐ Coleridge Road ⓣ 0114 223 5600 ⓦ www.eis-sheffield.co.uk ⓛ 07.00–21.00 Mon–Fri, 09.00–17.00 Sat & Sun ⓝ Tram: Arena/Don Valley Stadium

The Five Weirs Walk

This five-mile route gives walkers a feeling for Sheffield's industrial past that you simply can't get in a car or on a tram. It also gives a real insight into just how much the Don Valley corridor has changed following the huge post-industrial cleanup operation. Spanning the distance between Lady's Bridge in the city centre and the Meadowhall Shopping Centre to the northeast, the route passes five weirs before joining a second trail that links it to the neighbouring town of Rotherham. Known as the river that came back from the dead, the Don is now home to a good deal of wildlife. Ⓦ www.fiveweirs.co.uk Ⓝ Tram: Fitzalan Square/Ponds Forge or Meadowhall Interchange

CULTURE

Don Valley Stadium

Like many of the sports facilities in Sheffield, the Don Valley Stadium was constructed for the 1991 World Student Games. Today it's still one of the biggest athletics stadiums in the UK, and is also used for open-air concerts, the British American Football League, and as the starting point for the annual Sheffield Half Marathon. It's an impressive structure made up of giant white tents stretched between equally large and easily recognisable yellow pylons. Ⓐ Leeds Road Ⓣ 0114 223 3600 Ⓦ www.donvalleystadium.co.uk Ⓔ info@donvalleystadium.co.uk Ⓝ Tram: Arena/Don Valley Stadium

Ice Sheffield

A short walk from Sheffield Arena, Ice Sheffield contains two Olympic-sized ice rinks for recreational fun, curling and ice hockey tuition, among other activities. It opened in 2003 and has become extremely popular with beginners and professional skaters alike. Ⓐ Coleridge Road Ⓣ 0114 223 3900

'The Big Melt', one of Magna's most breathtaking exhibits

Ⓦ www.icesheffield.com Ⓔ info@icesheffield.com
Ⓛ Recreational skating hours vary, call to check Ⓝ Tram: Arena/
Don Valley Stadium

Magna Science Adventure Centre
Based in what used to be the old Templeborough Steelworks,
this science centre is a lot of fun no matter how old you are. The
areas inside are split into hands-on exhibitions demonstrating
the awesome power of the four elements. The five-metre-tall fire
tornado is a big draw, as are the exploding rock face, the gigantic
steel water wheel and the huge Zeppelin airship up in the
rafters. There's also a great screen show documenting how steel
created the community in Sheffield. Ⓐ Sheffield Road Ⓣ 01709
720 002 Ⓦ www.visitmagna.co.uk Ⓔ info@magnatrust.co.uk
Ⓛ 10.00–17.00 daily Ⓘ Admission charge

Sheffield Arena
This is the proud home of the Sheffield Steelers ice hockey team,
as well as being Sheffield's largest indoor concert venue, with a
staggering 13,500-person capacity and a fantastically diverse
events calendar. From the indoor International Supercross or
Riverdance to Lady Gaga or comedian Peter Kay, you'll find
something on the bill to suit your tastes and timetable.
Ⓐ March St Ⓣ 0114 256 5656 Ⓦ www.sheffieldarena.co.uk
Ⓝ Tram: Arena/Don Valley Stadium

Valley Centertainment
One of the most popular spots in the area, Valley
Centertainment somewhat resembles an outdoor shopping

centre, but instead of shops you'll find a huge multi-screen cinema, an American-style bowling alley and a collection of restaurants that'll leave you spoilt for choice. Valley Centertainment has a dedicated tram stop and there's plenty of parking in the complex, too. ⓐ Broughton Lane ⓦ www.valley-leisure.co.uk ⓝ Tram: Valley Centertainment

RETAIL THERAPY

Meadowhall Shopping Centre

At the end of the Don Valley corridor lies Meadowhall – a beacon of regeneration in an area formerly dominated by the Hadfield Steelworks. Twenty years old in 2010, this indoor mall has everything the modern shopper needs. At its core is the Oasis Food Court, a huge eating area under a glass dome surrounded by dozens of charming little shops in the Lanes. The Oasis also leads to a multi-screen cinema and the two huge wings of the complex. These wings house more than 270 shops and countless brands, spread out over more than 140,000 sq m (1.5 million sq ft). Meadowhall also has its own transport hub to accommodate the 25 million shoppers who walk through its doors every year. Trains, trams, buses and National Express coaches all have dedicated stops here and there are more than 12,000 free parking spaces for cars driving in from the nearby M1 motorway. ⓐ Meadowhall Road ⓣ 0114 256 8800 ⓦ www.meadowhall.co.uk ⓒ 10.00–21.00 Mon–Fri, 09.00–19.00 Sat, 11.00–17.00 Sun ⓝ Tram: Meadowhall Interchange

Meadowhall Retail Park

If you were to take the contents of the Meadowhall Shopping Centre, shake them up, remove the roof over the connecting corridors and replace the large department stores with toy shops and domestic furnishers, then you'd get the Meadowhall Retail Park. It's a ten-minute drive or Supertram ride away from the mall and shoppers here have access to around 30 shops. The focus is geared towards the home, gardening, pets and a toy shop the size of a Premier League football field. 🄰 Attercliffe Common 🄽 Tram: Carbrook

TAKING A BREAK

Meadowhall Shopping Centre 🄻 🄰 Meadowhall Road 🕒 See page 73. Certain bars and licensed restaurants are open until 23.00 Sat and 22.30 Sun

Café Nova £ There are lots of café stands dotted around in the walkways of Meadowhall but if you fancy sitting down for a cup of tea and a slice of cake in a place with doors and walls, then Café Nova is for you. You can find it on the upper level, near the Debenhams department store.
☎ 0144 256 9485

Chilango £ A top-notch Mexican kitchen in the Oasis Food Court where burritos, tacos, totopos and salsa abound. The margaritas are pretty good, too – especially if you feel like a treat after a hard day's shopping. ☎ 0144 256 9031

Handmade Burger Co. £–££ The title of this eatery says it all. The staggering array of beef, chicken, lamb, fish and vegetarian burgers on the menu are all made to order and served in freshly baked bread buns. ☎ 0144 256 8945

Zizzi ££ This restaurant on the upper level of the Oasis Food Court serves up generous portions of authentic Italian cuisine. It's also a good spot for a break if you feel the need for some breathing room between you and the throngs of shoppers making pit stops for fast food on the lower level. ☎ 0144 251 6777

Valley Centertainment ⓲ ⓐ Broughton Lane ⏰ See venues below:

The Boardwalk Roadhouse £–££ This bar and grill is very family friendly and all about the cheerful tunes pumped out

▲ *Catch a Supertram to Valley Centertainment*

onto the surrounding pavements. Expect a hearty menu with an American theme. ☎ 0114 243 5438 ⓦ www.boardwalk-restaurant.co.uk 🕐 12.00–21.00 Sun–Fri, 12.00–22.00 Sat

Flaming Dragon £–££ In the 2008 Eat Sheffield Awards, this place took the gong in the best Asian and Oriental food category, and the food served here remains among the best in the city. ☎ 0144 244 9866 🕐 12.00–23.00 Mon–Thur, 12.00–24.00 Fri & Sat, 12.00–22.30 Sun

Old Orleans Restaurant ££ If you like gumbo and jambalaya, then it's worth stopping for a bite to eat at this American South-themed restaurant. ☎ 0114 244 6667 ⓦ www.oldorleans.com 🕐 12.00–21.00 Sun–Fri, 11.30–21.30 Sat

AFTER DARK

Between them, Sheffield Arena, the Don Valley Arena, Ice Sheffield and the English Institute of Sport host all of the shows and sporting events that you could hope for in this area. On certain occasions Ice Sheffield also hosts ice-skating discos with DJs.

There are a few pubs dotted around Carbook and Attercliffe, but rather than really going out in this part of the city, most Sheffielders would choose to hop on a tram to the centre – a mere ten-minute ride away.

▶ *Monsal Head in the Peak District*

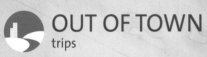

OUT OF TOWN
trips

Peak District

Ask anyone in Sheffield about the Golden Frame and they'll proudly tell you that this refers to the unspoilt countryside surrounding most of the city – namely the Peak District. The term can be traced back to the pollution of the industrial age, when the nearby fresh air and unpolluted landscapes were a welcome break from the soot and grime of the inner city. In fact, the area was so cherished that the people of Sheffield took it upon themselves to protect it by applying for National Park status. It took nearly 25 years for this to become a reality, but in 1951 the Peak District National Park became the first in Britain. Today, city residents and world travellers visit the park to enjoy the many beautiful sights and historic landmarks. From Neolithic rock formations rivalling Stonehenge to the splendour of Chatsworth House, the Peak District is brimming with top attractions and a rich cultural legacy.

GETTING THERE

By bus Local buses are an extremely efficient way of getting to the Peak District. The 218 from Sheffield city centre, for example, will get you to the town of Bakewell in just under 45 minutes.

By car Take the A621 from Sheffield straight down to Baslow. This 30-minute drive puts you in a prime position for exploring all of the attractions nearby.

Bakewell's idyllic setting

SIGHTS & ATTRACTIONS

To narrow down the best bits of this 1,425-sq-km (550-sq-miles) national park, a good starting point is the White Peak. This southern area of the park gets its name from its lightly coloured limestone.

Bakewell

To many, this attractive little market town is the heart of the Peak District. The perfectly preserved shops, stone fronted cottages and quaint tea rooms combine to make Bakewell the perfect getaway. The **Visitor Centre** between Buxton Road and Bridge Street offers visitors top tips about the best **Bakewell Pudding** in town, the award winning **Old House Museum**, the **weekly street markets** and the work of the **National Park Authority** based in the area. Afternoon tea is a rite of passage in Bakewell, so if you only do one thing here, make sure it involves a cup of tea, a scone, some clotted cream and a good splodge of jam.

The Nine Ladies Stone Circle and Arbor Low

The Nine Ladies Stone Circle is an ancient monument dating from more than 4,000 years ago. According to local legend the stones represent a group of women who angered God by dancing on Sunday and were consequently turned to stone. This attraction is on Stanton Moor, a short distance away from Arbor Low, another interesting Neolithic stone formation known to many as the Stonehenge of the North.
ⓦ www.englishheritage.org.uk

Walking trails

There are many signposted trails crisscrossing the Peak District, including the High Peak Trail, the Manifold Track, the Tissington Trail, the Longdendale Trail and the Monsal Trail, which begins near Bakewell. Detailed information for all routes can be found in local visitor centres.

CULTURE

Chatsworth House

The great dining rooms, art-filled hallways and painted ceilings of this stately home, which served as a prison to Mary, Queen of Scots before she was transferred to Sheffield Castle, are some of the finest in the country. Today, the events calendar includes fairs, horse trials, car rallies, the *Antiques Roadshow*, sculpture exhibitions and more. The gardens, maze and farmyard are also popular and well suited to young families. For a nice hike nearby, ask about the circuit encompassing the Hunting Tower, Swiss Cottage, Beeley Hilltop Farm, Hell Bank Plantation and the kissing gate at Carlton Lees. ☏ 01246 565 300 ⓦ www.chatsworth.org ⓔ visit@chatsworth.org 🕐 11.00–17.30 daily ⓘ Admission charge

The Old House Museum

Just behind the Parish Church in Bakewell, this atmospheric museum is captivating for children and adults alike, offering a look back at life in the town over the past 500 years. ⓐ Cunningham Place ☏ 01629 813 642 ⓦ www.oldhousemuseum.co.uk 🕐 11.00–16.00 daily (Apr–Oct), closed Nov–Mar ⓘ Admission charge

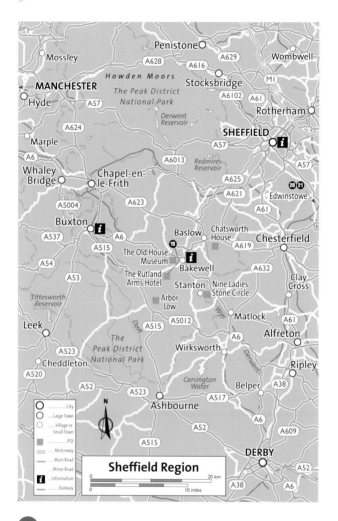

Sheffield Region

RETAIL THERAPY

To pick up a local memento try the **weekly street market** that takes over the square behind the Visitor Centre in Bakewell every Monday. Alternatively, take a taste of the Peak District away with you courtesy of **The Old Original Bakewell Pudding Shop**. Here you can buy a Bakewell Pudding (not a tart) and find out all about how this local delicacy was created by mistake at a dinner party held at the nearby Rutland Arms Hotel. The guests at this party allegedly included Annie Wilson, the original shop owner who passed the secret recipe down through the ages.

TAKING A BREAK

The Old Original Bakewell Pudding Shop £ ⑲ The ingredients of the dessert sold here are top secret, but there's no better accompaniment to a nice pot of tea. ⓐ The Square ⓣ 01629 812 193 ⓦ www.bakewellpuddingshop.co.uk ⓛ 09.00–18.00 daily (shop); 09.00–17.30 daily (restaurant)

ACCOMMODATION

The Rutland Arms Hotel ££–£££ A charming local hotel full of 19th-century knick-knacks and local charm, this is the reputed birthplace of the Bakewell Pudding, not to mention a favourite bolt-hole of Jane Austen – she reputedly stayed here while writing *Pride and Prejudice*. ⓐ The Square ⓣ 01629 812 812 ⓦ www.rutlandarmsbakewell.com ⓔ enquiries@rutlandbakewell.co.uk

Sherwood Forest & Clumber Park

The legendary home of Robin Hood is less than an hour away from Sheffield. This 466-sq-km (180-sq-mile) protected area contains the ancient Major Oak, a state-of-the-art Visitor Centre, exciting off-road access and, at its northernmost point, Clumber Park. Sherwood Forest makes for a great day trip, picnic spot or festival venue, and the journey there from Sheffield is pretty picturesque, too. If you like hiking, cycling, horse riding and the great outdoors, you'll like Sherwood Forest.

GETTING THERE

By bus Take a National Express coach from Sheffield Interchange to Mansfield. Then take a local bus to Edwinstone, which is a short taxi ride or a ten-minute walk away from the Visitor Centre.

By car Head straight down the M1 and take the A57 exit at Junction 21. Follow the directions for Worksop and Carburton, where signposts for Clumber Park and Sherwood Forest start. There is metered parking at the Visitor Centre and in Clumber Park.

Useful websites:
www.sherwoodforest.org.uk
www.newark-sherwooddc.gov.uk
www.nationaltrust.org.uk

SIGHTS & ATTRACTIONS

Sherwood Forest National Nature Reserve and Visitor Centre

This reserve covers more than 182 hectares (450 acres) of Robin Hood's old stomping ground and includes the ancient (and propped up) Major Oak. This tree is said to be more than 800 years old and a former place of shelter for Mr Hood and his band of merry men. At the state-of-the-art Visitor Centre there's information about the many signposted walks through the forest, the annual Robin Hood Summer Festival, a variety of exhibitions examining the history of the forest and listings for the open air theatre. ⓐ Edwinstone ⓣ 01623 823 202 ⓦ www.nottinghamshire.gov.uk/sherwoodforestcp

🔺 *Robin Hood's lair? The Major Oak*

🔵 sherwood.forest@nottscc.gov.uk 🕐 Country Park dawn–dusk daily, Visitor Centre 10.00–17.00 daily (Apr–Oct), 10.00–16.30 daily (Nov–Mar)

Clumber Park

This old country estate was left to the people of Worksop by the Dukes of Newcastle before the National Trust stepped in, bought the land and made it into the attraction it is today. Within the 1,540 hectares (3,800 acres) of parkland you'll find many walking routes, a dedicated climbing forest and scores of wildlife conservation areas teeming with local creatures and hands-on activities. 🕐 Estate Office 01909 544 917 🔵 www.nationaltrust.org.uk/clumberpark 🔵 clumberpark@nationaltrust.org.uk

Clumber Park Cycle Hire Centre The park contains more than 30 km (20 miles) of cycle routes through its spectacular scenery, as well as a handy Cycle Centre where you can hire a pair of wheels for the day – or you can bring your own. 🕐 10.00–17.00 daily (Apr–Oct), 10.00–16.00 Sat & Sun, closed Mon–Fri (Nov–Mar)

Clumber Chapel Much of the aristocratic architecture in the grounds of Clumber Park was lost to fire, demolition, the two World Wars and economic depression, but some of the grandeur endured – including the Grade I listed Clumber Chapel. This Neo-Gothic style building is considered by many to be a miniature cathedral, and the ornately decorated interior is definitely worth seeing. 🕐 10.00–17.00 daily (Apr–Oct), 10.00–16.00 daily (Nov–Mar)

Clumber Park – Walled Kitchen Garden This garden gives visitors a true taste of the past and the chance to see the restored glasshouses, vegetable plots and vineyards that once supplied the estate. 🕐 10.00–17.00 daily (Apr–Oct), 10.00–16.00 daily (Nov–Mar)

CULTURE

Sherwood Forest Farm Park

Expect more than mere farm animals at this 11-hectare (27-acre) reserve. The farm is most certainly family orientated, providing interest for all ages. ⓐ Lamb Pens Farm, Edwinstowe ⓣ 01623 823 558 ⓦ www.sherwoodforestfarmpark.co.uk 🕐 10.30–17.15 daily (Apr–Sept), closed Oct–Mar ⓘ Admission charge

The Clumber Story

A collection of exhibitions offering a fascinating insight into the history of the park, how it came into existence and how it was used as a top-secret military base, test site and ammunitions depot during World War II. 🕐 10.00–17.00 daily (Apr–Oct), 10.00–16.00 daily (Nov–Mar)

RETAIL THERAPY

As you'd expect in the great outdoors, there aren't many shopping opportunities. There is, however, the **Robin Hood Shop** selling mementoes and souvenirs at the **Sherwood Forest National Nature Reserve and Visitor Centre**. Much of what is sold here benefits the National Trust.

TAKING A BREAK

The Café in Sherwood Forest £ 🄩 Attached to an arts and crafts centre, this charming little café serves up takeaway forest picnics, hearty breakfasts, a good sandwich menu and has Wi-Fi internet access. There's also a relaxed coffee lounge, popular with walkers seeking a spot of quiet contemplation. 🄰 Forest Corner, Edwinstowe 🄣 01623 824 033 🄦 www.stop4t.co.uk 🄴 info@stop4t.co.uk 🄲 10.00–17.00 Tues–Sun, closed Mon (Apr–Sept), 10.00–16.00 Wed–Sun, closed Mon & Tues (Oct–Mar)

Launay's Restaurant ££ 🄬 Within easy walking distance of Sherwood Forest, this 16th-century cottage has been converted into a comfortable and intimate eatery, serving up a selection of local and international dishes. 🄰 Church Street, Edwinstowe 🄣 01623 822 268 🄦 www.launaysrestaurant.co.uk 🄲 12.00–15.00 & 18.30–22.00 Mon–Sat, 12.00–16.00 Sun

ACCOMMODATION

Clumber Park Hotel and Spa £–££ A great location and a good choice of rooms for solo travellers, couples, families and groups. There's a luxury spa attached and special offers are regularly available. 🄰 Blyth Road, Clumber Park 🄣 01623 835 333 🄦 www.clumberparkhotel.com 🄴 gm@clumberparkhotel.com

🄳 *The Tourist Information Centre, Norfolk Row*

PRACTICAL
information

Directory

GETTING THERE
By air

Just 25 miles away, Robin Hood Airport Doncaster Sheffield is easily accessible from Sheffield. From the airport flights connect to more than 40 international destinations.

Aer Lingus 🕿 0871 718 5000 🆆 www.aerlingus.com
easyJet 🕿 0871 244 2366 🆆 www.easyjet.com
Thomas Cook 🕿 0871 230 2406 🆆 http://book.flythomascook.com
Wizz Air 🕿 0906 959 0002 🆆 www.wizzair.com

With many of the operators at Robin Hood Airport, it's possible to offset your carbon footprint by paying an additional fee. You can find out more about this on the individual airline websites or by visiting 🆆 www.robinhoodairport.com

Many people are aware that air travel emits CO_2, which contributes to climate change. You may be interested in the possibility of lessening the environmental impact of your flight through the charity **Climate Care** (🆆 www.jpmorganclimatecare.com), which offsets your CO_2 by funding environmental projects around the world.

By road

A car isn't essential for making the most of Sheffield, but the city is well connected to the UK's road infrastructure. The M1 is the primary access road and the Parkway dual carriageway takes drivers straight into the city centre.

By rail

Sheffield is well served by the railway, being on a number of
cross-country routes, as well as having branch line connections
to high-speed rail links. All timetables and destinations linked to
Sheffield by rail, can be found on the Network Rail website.
Ⓦ www.nationalrail.co.uk

By bus

All travel information regarding bus routes across Sheffield and
South Yorkshire can be found on the regularly updated displays
at the Sheffield Interchange bus station, as well as online.
Ⓦ www.travelsouthyorkshire.com

GETTING AROUND

You can get a taxi from the ranks outside the train station
and the City Hall. For advance bookings, Sheffield City Taxis
are a good company to use. ❶ 0114 239 3939
Ⓦ www.sheffieldcitytaxis.com

If you want to hire a car, your best bet is City Car Club
(Ⓦ www.citycarclub.co.uk) who make vehicles available by
the hour, across the city. Alternatively try Europcar
(Ⓦ www.europcar.co.uk) or Hertz (Ⓦ www.hertz.com).

For full listings of local train and bus routes, including up-
to-date timetables and itinerary–specific planning, visit
Ⓦ www.travelsouthyorkshire.com

For all travel-related enquiries call the dedicated
Traveline service on ❶ 01709 515151. For more details
regarding the Sheffield Supertram network visit
Ⓦ www.supertram.com

HEALTH, SAFETY AND CRIME

The main hospital in Sheffield is the Northern General on Herries Road (☎ 0114 243 4343). There are also a good number of general practitioners across the city, including the Sheffield City GP Health Centre (☎ 0114 241 2700). If you need the police, you can find the South Yorkshire Police Headquarters on Snig Hill in the city centre (☎ 0114 220 2020).

OPENING HOURS

The shops in Sheffield are generally open 09.00–18.00 Mon–Sat, with slightly shorter opening hours on a Sunday. Banks are normally open 09.00–17.00 Mon–Fri and 09.00–12.00 on Saturdays. They are closed on Sundays. The main museums in the city are usually open 10.00–17.00 Mon–Sat, closing slightly earlier on Sundays.

TOILETS

In the city centre, there are public toilets and baby changing facilities in the lower level of the Millennium Gallery, directly behind the escalators. In Attercliffe and Carbrook, there are a good number of facilities available in the Meadowhall Shopping Centre, while in the Ecclesall Road area, public toilets are available in Endcliffe Park and in the Weston Park Museum.

CHILDREN

Many of the activities and attractions in Sheffield are suited to children, but the following selection is specifically geared towards a younger audience:

Magna Science Adventure Centre A fantastic, interactive science centre where children of all ages learn all about the elements through the interactive exhibits (see page 72).

Monkey Business Expect ball pits, organised fun and much more at this play centre, located in the Centertainment area. The attractions here are aimed primarily at children under the age of seven. ⓐ Broughton Lane ⓣ 08458 739 645 ⓦ www.monkey-bizness.co.uk ⓔ sheffield@monkey-bizness.co.uk

TRAVELLERS WITH DISABILITIES

Sheffield is a mixed bag for anyone with mobility problems. Many of the areas and facilities created and regenerated by the Heart of the City Project are completely accessible, but some of the older and more remote buildings can prove to be less so.

The Supertram network is wheelchair-friendly, as are many of the attractions that it visits – including Meadowhall and Valley Centertainment. You can find out more information about relevant facilities by visiting ⓦ www.sheffield.gov.uk

There are a number of wheelchair-friendly taxi firms operating in Sheffield, including the aforementioned Sheffield City Taxis. ⓣ 0114 239 3939 ⓦ www.sheffieldcitytaxis.com

FURTHER INFORMATION

The Tourist Information Centre for Sheffield is located at ⓐ 14 Norfolk Row ⓣ 0114 221 1900 ⓦ www.yorkshiresouth.com ⓔ visitor@yorkshiresouth.com ⓛ 10.00–17.00 Mon–Fri, 10.00–16.00 Sat, closed Sun

ACKNOWLEDGEMENTS
The photographs in this book were taken by the Thomas Cook Photography Team for Thomas Cook Publishing, to whom the copyright belongs, except for the following: Craig Fleming page 49; iStockphoto pages 77 (Ann Taylor-Hughes), 79 (Mike Dabell), 85 (mikeuk); Magna Science Adventure Centre page 71; Museums Sheffield page 51 (Adrian Richardson); Sheffield Botanical Gardens page 59; Sheffield Ski Village page 21; Valley Centertainment Sheffield page 75; Weston Park Museums page 29 (Adrian Richardson).

Project editor: Tom Lee
Copy editor: Jennifer Jahn
Proofreaders: Emma Haigh & Michele Greenbank
Layout: Julie Crane
Indexer: Penelope Kent

AUTHOR BIOGRAPHY
Robert Savage is in the British Guild of Travel Writers and backpacks around the world, writing for magazines and guidebooks. In his home city of Sheffield he enjoys drinking coffee at 22A Norfolk Row, perusing the art collections at the Graves Gallery and scouting out the next big bands at The Boardwalk.

Send your thoughts to
books@thomascook.com

- Found a great bar, club, shop or must-see sight that we don't feature?
- Like to tip us off about any information that needs a little updating?
- Want to tell us what you love about this handy little guidebook and more importantly how we can make it even handier?

Then here's your chance to tell all! Send us ideas, discoveries and recommendations today and then look out for your valuable input in the next edition of this title.

Email the above address (stating the title) or write to:
pocket guides Series Editor, Thomas Cook Publishing, PO Box 227, Coningsby Road, Peterborough PE3 8SB, UK.